DENVER
COMES OF AGE

DENVER
COMES OF AGE

The Postwar Photography of
Morey Engle

JOHNSON BOOKS: BOULDER

9 8 7 6 5 4 3 2 1

Cover and text design by Bob Schram/Bookends

Library of Congress Cataloging-in-Publication Data
Engle, Morey, 1923–
    Denver comes of age : the postwar photography of Morey Engle /
Morey Engle.
        p.   cm.
    Includes index.
    ISBN 1-55566-115-7
    1. Denver (Colo.)—History—Pictorial works.   I. Title.
F784.D443E54   1994
978.8'83033'0222—dc20   94-32019
                                                                            CIP

Frontispiece
Morey Engle and the camera set-up he used to photograph the demolition of the Grant Smelter smokestack. February 25, 1950.

Printed in the United States by
Johnson Printing
1880 South 57th Court
Boulder, Colorado 80301

*Dedicated to my kids, Cathy, Bill, Morey, and Chris.
Over the years they have given me much happiness and pride in their
accomplishments. Life with them has never been dull.*

CONTENTS

FOREWORD

PEAK OF ACTION

It's called "peak of action"—an event frozen in time by the shutter of a newspaper photographer's camera. A split second earlier or later would miss it. Capturing that peak of action is the dream of every shooter, as newspaper photographers are called. Through the years they have been known as photogs, lensmen, and, more recently, as photo journalists. Apply any or all of those terms to Morey Engle, and they will fit.

In the almost fifty years I have worked with, around, and for Morey, I have never known anyone who had his instinct for capturing the peak of action. There's a photograph in this book that illustrates his hair-trigger instinct. Morey and I were walking away from the attempted destruction of the giant Grant Smelter stack in 1950. When the dust of the dynamite blast cleared, only half of the big brick stack had come down. Suddenly, we heard a sharp cracking noise. Morey whirled around and shot the picture with his Speed Graphic belly high, just as the remainder of the stack collapsed. He was the only one who got a picture.

Newspapers have changed since Morey's stint with the *Rocky Mountain News* between 1946 and 1956. Headlines were big and black, and photographs then were not just illustrations of stories, but of events actually taking place.

◀ Rocky Mountain News *photographer Morey Engle and reporter Jack Gaskie climb a fire department ladder truck to get to the peak of action.*

There were fires, plane crashes, train wrecks, gangland killings, floods, and other natural disasters. Morey covered them all. On many of those assignments, the city editor told him, "Either get the picture or you're fired."

That was hardball journalism in those days. The upstart *News* had to play it that way to compete with the rich and powerful *Denver Post*. People bought the *News* because they admired its spunk and liked the gritty coverage it offered. It was the perfect place to work for a kid who grew up in Denver and who freelanced as a photographer on a bicycle when he was still a student at East High.

The tool of the trade in those days was the 4x5 Speed Graphic, a far cry from today's 35mm Nikons with automatic shutters that shoot pictures like a machine gun. With the old Graphic, you had to get it right, sometimes with only one shot. Morey never fooled with complicated range finders. He cut notches in his camera so he could estimate distance even in the dark and feel with his thumb where to adjust the range.

Morey learned to fly during the war and used that skill many times to cover stories from the air. Somehow, he managed to fly the plane and take photographs with the old Speed Graphic at the same time. It seems strange now, but there was a dress code for photographers then. Shirt, tie, and coat were mandatory, even if you were sent out to cover a forest fire. Today's shooters dress as though they were going to clean the garage.

While at the *News,* Morey met, courted, and married Harriet Rhoads, also a newspaper photographer and daughter of Harry Rhoads, the dean of all Denver newspaper photographers. Morey edited *Denver's Man with a Camera: The Photographs of Harry Rhoads.* While Morey's book of photographs is different, it is a perfect historical companion to Harry's book. When you look at this pictorial retrospective, you will be transported back in time to that wonderful early postwar era when Denver was an exciting place to live and work. You'll see it as Morey saw it, through the lens of his old Speed Graphic.

Morey is retired now, but he still has a police scanner in his car and still carries a camera everywhere. If something happens, Morey will be there to capture the peak of action.

—*Gene Amole*

ACKNOWLEDGMENTS

The author wishes to acknowledge the invaluable assistance of the following people in the publication of this book: Lou Clinton, formerly of Clinton Aviation; M. J. Nichols, formerly of Clinton Aviation; Bill Fletcher, retired *Rocky Mountain News* chairman of the board; Larry Strutton, publisher of the *Rocky Mountain News*; Jay Ambrose, editor of the *Rocky Mountain News*; Janet Boss, *Rocky Mountain News* librarian; Eleanor Gehres and the staff of the Western History Department of the Denver Public Library; Kathy Swan, Denver Public Library; and Louise Myers for her assistance in research.

A very special thanks goes to Augie Mastrogiuseppe for finding my old negatives that the *Rocky Mountain News* gave to the Denver Public Library. A special thanks also goes to my good friend, Gene Amole, for his encouragement and support of this project.

And last, but certainly not least, my unending gratitude goes to my wife, Harriet, for her tireless and selfless editing and encouragement.

The photographs in this book were taken between 1939 and 1964, some as freelance assignments but many during my employment by the *Rocky Mountain News*, 1946–56. When known, the date of the photograph is included at the conclusion of the caption.

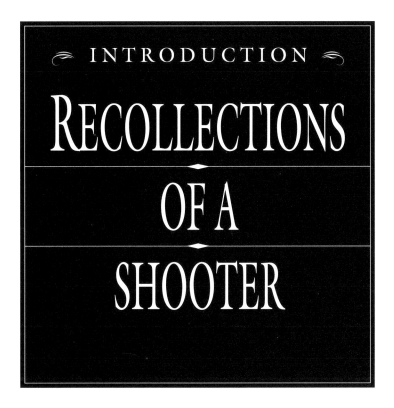

INTRODUCTION

RECOLLECTIONS OF A SHOOTER

I admit it. My long-time buddy, Gene Amole, called it just right when he said that I'm a shooter. That's all I ever really wanted to be. Since I was a kid rushing around Denver on my bicycle in the 1930s, I've had a camera with me wherever I've gone. It's taken me a lot of places and given me a close-up look at many scenes that few people get to experience—some funny, some tragic, some important, some part of everyday life. Wherever I've turned my camera lens, I've found the faces of Denver looking back at me.

My parents, Horace Samuel Engle and Lena Waldman, were married in Chicago, Illinois, on July 12, 1912. Mother had eleven miscarriages, and I turned out to be an only child. In 1922, Dad built a house at 736 Madison Street on Denver's east side. I was born Morris Adolph Engle on April 8, 1923, at Denver's Mercy Hospital. Early on, Morey replaced Morris except for official tag lines, Uncle Sam, and an occasional fellow looking for a fight.

I remember a happy childhood with neighborhood friends. One of the great things that city kids are missing today is the vacant lot. Across the street from our house were six vacant lots that had an embankment of four to five feet. We would go over and make roads on the side of the hill for toy cars and trucks and then excavate caves big enough for small towns. It was great fun.

◄ *This photograph of me was taken on the fire escape at the back of the old* Rocky Mountain News *building at 1720 Welton.*

Dad was financially independent during this period. We had a maid and Mother was quite involved socially with friends and card parties. Then, one mild October evening about 5:00, we got a shocker. Mother and I were on the porch waiting for Dad as usual. Dad walked up the steps, put his arms around Mother, and said, "Honey, we've lost everything we have but our home." It was the "Black Friday" of the 1929 stock market crash and, even as a little kid, I remember that night vividly. Overnight, our lifestyle changed. The maid was gone the next day and on Monday morning, Dad left in search of a job.

By now I was six years old. My cousin had a magazine route for *Liberty*, *Physical Culture*, and *True Story* magazines. She was my age and my aunt suggested that I could do the same thing. She sent a representative to see me and at the ripe old age of six, I became a magazine salesman. My cut on *Liberty* was one-and-a-half cents and around five cents for the others. At the time, *True Story* was considered taboo, and no one wanted to get caught reading it. I had one customer, a single school teacher, who had a standing order for it, but required that I deliver it after dark and never mention to anyone in the neighborhood that she took it. It was pretty tame stuff by today's standards.

I attended Henry M. Teller Elementary School at Eleventh and Garfield. Across the street from Teller was a corner vacant lot where we played marbles. We used to draw a circle in the dirt about three to four feet in diameter, and the players would put marbles in the center and then lag to a line drawn in the dirt to see who shot first. It was played two ways: for keeps and for fun. For keeps, the winner kept the other players' marbles. For fun, everybody got their marbles back. Trading was big business and "aggies" were a prize to be jealously guarded.

In time, our interests turned from toy trucks and playing kick the can to more mechanical pursuits. My friends and I built wooden boats from scrap orange crates and sailed them on City Park Lake. We crafted crude telegraph sets with the key from a coffee can lid, and we made model airplanes from balsa wood kits. Of course, every Depression-era kid remembers collecting bottle caps.

For my thirteenth birthday, my folks bought me a blue Schwinn bicycle. I was instantly determined to be a delivery boy. On the corner of Eighth Avenue and Colorado Boulevard there were two drug stores, Walter's, owned by

Here I am hard at work—or at least looking like it!

Walter Risch, and Aylard's Drug. I went to see Mr. Risch and asked for a job. He already had a delivery boy, but needed a curb service boy, sort of a forerunner to the drive-in car-hop. I got the job and went to work at 6:00 PM and worked until 9:00 PM. I sat on one of the old Coca-Cola wire chairs leaning against the wall on the Eighth Avenue side and when a car drove up, I would run out and take their order for ice cream sodas, cokes, or whatever. Sometimes, you got a tip—maybe a nickel or ten cents if you were really lucky. Sometimes, though, you got nothing, and it wasn't long before I was looking for a more steady source of income.

My parents had a friend who owned a clothing store in the 1700 block of Lawrence Street. I asked the owner for a job and he agreed to give me a chance to sweep out the store and learn to wrap packages. I got paid $3 a week for sweeping out every afternoon after school and on Saturday mornings until noon. I rode my bicycle all the way from school to the store

I'm ready to take-off for an aerial photo assignment sometime in the late 1940s.

and then back home. I got along fine with the sweeping, but seemed to have trouble tearing the wrapping paper the right size. Usually, it was too small. This upset the owner and he sent me across the street to Hilb Manufacturing Company and told me to ask Mr. Hilb for our paper stretcher, which had been loaned to him earlier. Mr. Hilb said he was sorry, but he had loaned it to another business up Seventeenth Street. So, I rode over to pick it up, but the proprietor said he had loaned it to yet another business. Finally, after about five stops, I got the message and amused all of the parties to my "education." I did learn to tear the paper the right size from then on.

When I received my first paycheck, I walked over to the Daniels & Fisher lunch counter to have it cashed. I ordered a Virginia baked ham sandwich, a piece of apple pie, and a Coke—all of which cost about seventy cents. This became a weekly ritual, but I quickly saved enough for my special purpose. I bought a "Univex" folding pocket-sized camera and some film and soon was taking pictures of Mother and Dad, the house, the dog, my friends, and whatever else caught my eye.

A little later, I moved up to an Argus "Model A" 35mm camera, but getting film developed proved expensive, so I bought an Eastman Kodak developing kit and learned to develop my own film and make contact prints. Enlargers were very expensive to a kid like me, so I built one using an Ovaltine can as the lamp housing.

With all of my tinkering, I also built a radio receiver that could pick up police calls. One Saturday, while listening to the police radio, a call came in about a drowning at Windsor Lake. I hopped on my bicycle with my Argus and rode like hell to get over there. The fire department was already there working on the young victim trying to restore his breathing. I shot a whole roll of 35mm film and returned home to call a friend of mine who knew someone at the *Denver Post*. He took the film to the paper and made the first sale of my photographs. Needless to say, getting cash from doing something I really enjoyed made a big impression and I resolved to chase more police calls.

During a Boy Scout circus at City Auditorium, I met a photographer, Paul Norine, who was making pictures of the event. He was using a 4x5 Speed Graphic, and it really caught my attention. I started talking to him about the camera and what he was doing. Even though he was nine years older than I, he agreed to teach me how to use the Speed Graphic, if I would build a police adapter for his car radio. Thus began the apprenticeship. Paul did lots of commerical photography, and I spent much time with him on assignments when I wasn't in school.

By now I was attending East High School and had gotten my driver's license. I became the official photographer for the school newspaper and the annual. East had a 4x5 Graphic and I was able to squeeze in some of my own photography with it on weekends. Then during the summer of my junior year, I went to work at Colorado General Hospital washing dishes to earn enough money to buy my own Speed Graphic. The hours were from 5:45 AM until 9:00 PM or later if there was a conference in the dining room, and the pay was $65 a month, plus meals and laundry. I stayed two-and-a-half months, which gave me enough money for the camera with a bit to spare.

One evening, Paul Norine called me and said that he wanted to talk. Much to my surprise, he told me that he was getting married and leaving town and wondered if I would take over his commercial photo accounts. Needless to say, I was delighted, but from then on my school work suffered because I was more interested in photography.

Nonetheless, I managed to graduate from East High in 1941, and then had full-time to devote to building a commercial photography business. Evelyn Jones, a school teacher who lived across the street from us, asked me to take the photographs for a book she and two other teachers were writing. It was a textbook for young boys called *Boys Will Be Men*. It was one of my first big photography jobs and I felt good about it, being a kid just out of high school.

Everybody's world changed on December 7, 1941, and I enlisted in the Army Air Corps shortly afterward. After basic training, I started flight training, but in the middle, the flight schools became so overloaded with students that some of us were temporarily sent home. I spent three months of 1942 working as a clerk in the radio room at the Denver Police Department before being called back to finish my training. Eventually, I spent time at Lowry Field as a photo instructor and was ultimately discharged at Fort Sheridan, Illinois. I worked for the U.S. Army Signal Corps in Dayton, Ohio, for a time, but then my dad became ill so I returned to Denver and started freelance photography work again.

Denver was much the same as it had been at the beginning of the war, but there were certainly signs that this was going to change. It seemed as if nearly everyone who had spent any time at all in Colorado during the war now wanted to move here. I had taken photographs for one of Mayor Ben Stapleton's earlier campaigns. In the fall of 1946, after almost twenty years as mayor, Stapleton was asked how Denver was going to deal with the problems all of the newcomers would create. He looked out of the window of the mayor's office and answered, "If these people would just go back where they came from, we wouldn't have any problems here." The following June, in a classic changing of the guard, Quigg Newton, a navy veteran half Stapleton's age, was elected mayor of Denver.

Newton presided over Denver as mayor for two terms. Those eight years and the remainder of the 1950s saw many changes take place in Denver. Increased federal spending,

My main tool of the trade was my trusty 4x5 Graphic.

recreational developments in the mountains to the west, burgeoning local industries, sprawling suburbs, and an increasingly mobile population all brought massive changes. I hired on with the *Rocky Mountain News* early in 1946 and spent those same years covering those events and everything else from new building construction to airplane crashes, snowstorms, and floods to grisly murders, and sporting events to heated political campaigns. It was a time of boom, but it was also a quieter time which today nostalgically seems to be the "good old days." Take a look with me and I'll show you what I mean.

ONE

SCENES FROM THE "GOOD OLD DAYS"

After the war, I returned to Denver and started freelancing again. I met up with old friends, some of whom, like police detective Jack Hargraves, helped me make contacts that got me hot tips on all kinds of breaking news stories. Freelance assignments were good, but I needed a steady income. I approached the *Rocky Mountain News* for a job, but they didn't have any openings.

A little while later, after buying some of my freelance photos, the *News* asked me to come in and offered me a job for $44 a week. I had a little daughter to support, so I said that I couldn't work for that salary. That ended the interview. A week later, City Editor Gene Lowall called and asked if I would work for $52 a week. I accepted.

During the years that followed, I covered just about every assignment imaginable for the *News*. There were Memorial Day parades and early November blizzards, hit-and-run accidents and labor disputes. I went to schools and sporting events, shootings and shopping center openings. I saw Denver through the sprawling panoramas I shot from the air and through reflective photos of contemplative kids. It's a great city and it's been a real kick watching it grow up. For me, those really were the "good old days."

◄ *Four Park Hill youngsters beat the heat with cool water from a fire hydrant on a hot summer day. July 30, 1951.*

In the fall of 1940, the author, behind the wheel of a vintage 1929 Ford Model T, and Jim Light enjoy a little curbside service in front of the Pick-A-Rib at Colfax Avenue and Steele Street. The Pick-A-Rib was one of the early drive-in restaurants with curb service.

The Veterans of Foreign Wars dedicated Hale Parkway in honor of Brigadier General Irving Hale, the founder of the organization and a general of volunteers. Mayor Ben Stapleton is third from the right. October 21, 1941.

The Townsend Plan was a pension plan proposed by Dr. Francis E. Townsend of Long Beach, California. It provided that all citizens of the United States over the age of sixty years be paid $200 a month from funds collected from a two-percent national sales tax. Congress voted down the plan on June 1, 1939, but interest in the idea continued and the Seventh National Townsend Convention was held in Denver in 1941. From left to right are Denver Mayor Ben Stapleton, Dr. Francis E. Townsend, and Colorado Governor John C. Vivian. July 14, 1941.

World War I merchandise was still sold in several army/navy surplus stores. The night window display at the National Army Store, located at 1039 Seventeenth Street (Seventeenth and Curtis streets), advertised merchandise such as army weapons, used and new uniforms, civilian clothes, mess kits, first-aid kits, tents, shoes, and boots.

During World War II, the Community Chest was renamed the War Chest. In the background is the AAA building (American Automobile Association) at 1509 Cheyenne Place.

On V-J Day, September 2, 1945, a jublilant crowd of servicemen and citizens celebrated on Sixteenth Street around and on top of the East Thirteenth Avenue trolley. World War II was over and Denver would never be the same again.

Denver's 1949 Memorial Day parade passes down Sixteenth Street. Thousands lined the parade route while I caught the action from a perch between California and Welton streets. The parade was organized by the United Veterans Council and featured William R. Welsh of the United Spanish War Veterans as grand marshall. May 30, 1949.

The Veterans of Foreign Wars contingent marched down Sixteenth Street in front of the Gano-Downs clothing store in another Memorial Day parade.

The American Legion Band marched up Seventeenth Street during an Elks convention.

Minnie Shroyer, in the doorway chatting with one of her drivers, was the owner of Min's Cab Company, the only cab company in Denver to be owned by a black woman. One of the benefits of working for Min was that she made great southern fried chicken. The office was located on Welton Street across from the Roxy Theater.

East High School students in a Chevrolet convertible coupe with a rumble seat wait for their order at the Pick-A-Rib at Colfax Avenue and Steele Street.

The Trailways Bus Depot at Seventeenth and Glenarm streets was a busy place.

Police officer Morton Gottschalk sits upon his three-wheeler motorcycle. Note the signs for 3.2 beer and all-day parking for twenty-five cents.

It's not the young model who is Miss Denver, *but the motor launch that carried thousands of Denver youngsters and others around City Park Lake. The lady is Barbara Noren, a contestant in the National Press Photographers annual beauty contest. June 14, 1951.*

Snow removal from city streets has always been a concern in Denver, sometimes even becoming an issue in mayoral campaigns. I made these pictures of snow removal efforts after the big blizzard of November 1946.

The intersection of Eighteenth and Broadway was a mess on the night of November 4, 1946. The storm tied up traffic all over town. After I took this photograph, I went into the bar of the Cosmopolitan Hotel and spent the night. November 4, 1946.

Streets were slushy in front of the Denver Union Bus Depot at Seventeenth and Glenarm streets after a November snowstorm. The building on the left is the old Denver Club. November 7, 1946.

Although driving was hazardous, Denver was a postcard winter wonderland with snow-lined streets and snow-laden cars and trees, as shown in this view looking south on Sherman Street from East Sixteenth Avenue toward the Colorado State Capitol. January 2, 1949.

The mystery of death holds the attention of a small boy as he ponders the lifeless body of "Bootsy," a neighborhood pet run over by a car. Another neighborhood canine stands guard over the body of his playmate. March 25, 1949.

At 9:50 PM on May 10, 1948, it was ten minutes to quitting time and the city editor sent Tom Gavin and me to cover a hit-and-run accident at Fifteenth and Clarkson. Figuring that it was a waste of time that close to deadline, we weren't happy to go, but on arriving we saw this man sitting on the curb. I got the camera and took a couple of shots and Tom got what he could for his story. It wasn't until I developed the pictures that I noticed that the poor man's leg was broken and off to one side. It was a very dark night and I hadn't seen the extent of his injuries. The man was a sixty-year-old itinerant from Santa Fe, New Mexico, who had been struck and dragged by a hit-and-run driver. After seeing this photograph in the newspaper the next day, a twenty-eight-year-old driver turned himself in to police. Not only did the photograph solve the case, but it also won an honorable mention in Denver Press Club News Photo Awards. Ten minutes to quitting time or not, you never knew when you were going to get one of the great ones. May 10, 1948.

◄

Neither Vernon Hale nor his pet dalmatian, Trixie, looks very happy. Trixie was run over by a car and suffered a broken leg. Vernon broke his arm while running to aid his pet. June 12, 1946.

This Easter photo of a young girl surrounded by little chicks won an honorable mention in Life magazine's contest for young photographers in 1951.

Cleo, the lioness at City Park Zoo, admits a "girdle gives a girl a certain something around the middle," but she got into the encircling tire by accident and it took zoo keepers more than an hour to release her. February 16, 1952.

Gunnison cattleman, later to be Colorado governor, Dan Thornton displayed his prize-winning bulls in the lobby of the Brown Palace Hotel, an event which quickly entered into the oft-told legends of the Brown. The bulls brought a record price of $50,000 each at the National Western Stockshow. January 19, 1945.

"Get a horse" might well be the battle cry of this belligerent cow, as she gives Denver patrolman Harry Werkmeister the eye. She was the last of a number of stray cattle to be rounded up in southwest Denver. March 24, 1952.

National Press Photographers Association members (left to right) Ira Sealy and Floyd McCall of the Denver Post, Morey Engle of the Rocky Mountain News, and Willard Haselbush of the Denver Post judge a photo contest for the association. March 15, 1952.

Miss Elsie Ward operates the telephone switchboard at the old Rocky Mountain News office at 1720 Welton.

The city newsroom in the then "new" Rocky Mountain News *building at 400 West Colfax was a spacious place in the days before computers and multi-line telephones. June 2, 1952.*

The composing room in the new Rocky Mountain News *building featured state-of-the-art typesetting with Linotype machines. June 2, 1952.*

The grand opening of a Miller's
Super Market featured an on-
site broadcast by Perry Allen
of radio station KTLN.

KIMN reporter and broadcaster
Don Martin (right) was on
hand for the opening of an
Arlans Department Store
in 1962.

Window shopping was an important part of Christmas for all of us, as these children peering in the window of Daniels & Fisher from Sixteenth Street can attest.

More than one thousand Swift and Armour Company employees, members of the United Packing House Workers, staged a gate rally to protest the inaction of the Wage Stabilization Board in approving a nine-cent per hour wage increase. February 13, 1951.

Arthur Nielson philosophically takes the flood waters in stride as he goes about the daily round of milk deliveries. Bare feet and rolled-up pants were the solution to the miniature lake he had to wade through. August 4, 1951.

When a storm blew through Denver in early August 1951, the News rushed to cover it and published this photograph of me with boots afoot and notepad and camera in hand, interviewing kids about what the storm did to their block. August 2, 1951.

Workmen from the Public Service Company check for gas leaks under the street about 1947.

Head-in angle parking was permitted on Broadway between Seventeenth and Eighteenth streets when this photograph was taken. The Brown Palace is on the left and a Sears Roebuck store and the Blue Parrot Inn on the right. The Blue Parrot was one of Denver's popular restaurants and featured a talking parrot in the entrance. November 7, 1946.

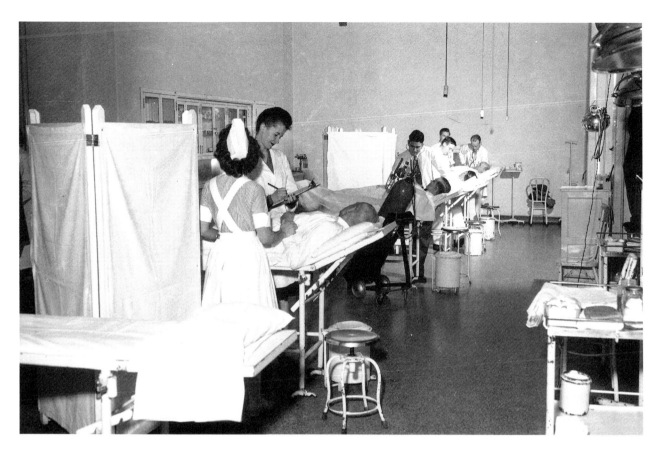

Compared to modern technology, the emergency room of Denver General Hospital was bare bones in this 1947 photograph.

A beer sale at the Plaza Liquor Store on Fifteenth Street limited customers to two bottles and offered Tivoli and Walter's beers, two of Colorado's many local beers.

I've always liked night shots. This one looks along Sixteenth Street, decorated for Christmas, sometime in the late 1940s.

Curtis Street, Denver's version of the "great white way," glistens with lights and rain in the season's first rainfall. On the left side are the Gem and Isis theaters, and on the right is the Colorado Candy Company. March 5, 1949.

The season's first rainfall made mirrors of Denver streets and turned most of the downtown section into a deserted city. This photograph was taken at Sixteenth Street looking south on Broadway. March 5, 1949.

Marines of the First 155mm Gun Battalion take advantage of a momentary delay of their troop train by exchanging last fond hugs and kisses with their wives, sweethearts, and children. The Marine Gun Battalion pulled out of Denver Union Station for further training on the West Coast. This was the first reserve unit from Colorado to be called to active duty for possible service in Korea. August 3, 1950.

A nun admits two children to the Margery Reed Mayo Day Nursery, at 1128 Twenty-eighth Street. April 26, 1945.

The Wynken, Blynken, and Nod statue in Washington Park has been a long-time favorite with Denver children.

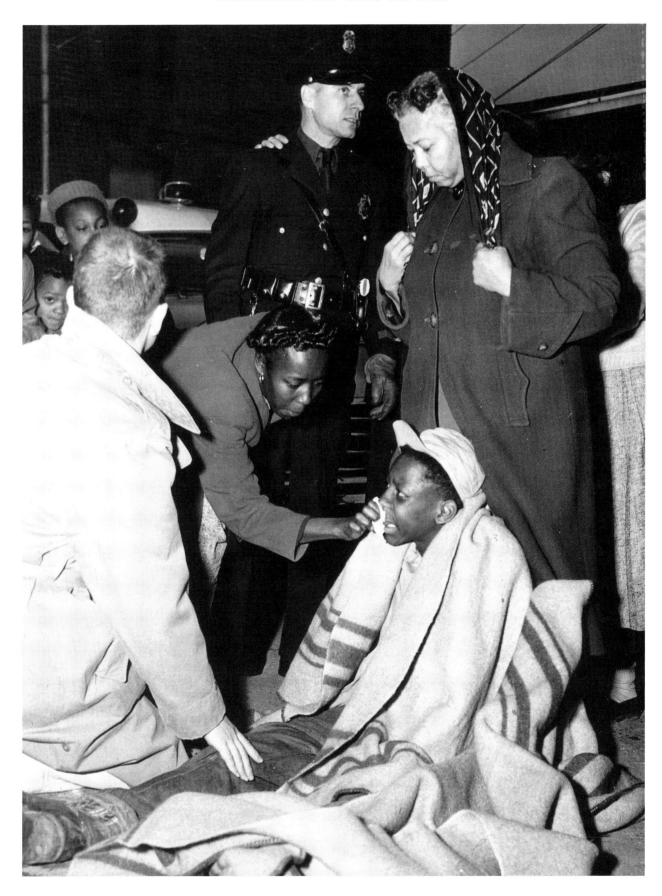

Thousands of dead fish floating in the Platte River provided a bonanza for these four boys, who collected more than a hundred big ones.

◄ *Mrs. Mary Paul wipes the tears from the eyes of her fourteen-year-old son, Jimmy, after the youth was struck by a car while riding his bicycle in the rear of his home at 2076 Ogden Street. The driver of the car told police he had no chance to stop when Jimmy darted from between two garages into the alley. Jimmy was taken to Denver General Hospital with a fractured right leg. March 5, 1952.*

I don't quite know how I did it, but I finally managed to get these seven boys to sit still long enough to make a picture. Good thing that I had a few toy trucks and planes on hand to keep them occupied. This picture was made as part of a fund-raising campaign for the Community Chest.

"School's out!" as I found out when the bell rang the last day of school at Teller Elementary. Even the teacher, Miss Ann Quigley, was happy to leave. Reporter Al Nakkula took the photograph and the camera and I survived the onslaught. June 6, 1952.

TWO

THE CHANGING
FACE OF
DENVER

Returning to Denver after the war, I found it much the same as I had left it—not too crowded and there was always a place to park downtown. The city was clean and pleasant, and the Daniels & Fisher Tower was still the tallest building in town. But most of this was soon to change. Venerable old landmarks were dwarfed by new skyscrapers throughout the 1950s, as I took photographs of Denver's changing skyline. Who could have foreseen then that the impressive heights of the First National Bank Tower, the Mile High Center, the Petroleum Club Building, and the original Security Life Building would all be dwarfed by another round of skyscraper construction in the early 1980s?

Photographing buildings was not always as safe as it might sound. When the steel girders were all in place on the University of Denver Law School building on Fourteenth Avenue across from the City and County Building, I was sent to make a picture of the traditional topping-out ceremony, complete with American flag on the highest point. I asked the foreman if there was a ladder to get up to where the flag raising was to be. He said, "Ride the hook up." I declined, and he said, "Just put your foot in the strap and see how it feels." Like a dummy I did, and the next thing I knew I was going skyward as the foreman gave the crane operator the high sign. I got off the hook, shot my pictures, climbed back down, and went looking for the foreman.

◀ *Denver Mayor Will Nicholson, third from left, and William Zeckendorf, far right, cut the ribbon for the opening of Zeckendorf Plaza on the old courthouse square at Sixteenth Street and Court Place. July 29, 1956.*

The old Denver City Hall at Fourteenth and Larimer streets was built in 1886 and was used by the police department after city offices moved to the City and County Building in 1932. This photograph was taken May 11, 1940.

The venerable Windsor Hotel on the corner of Eighteenth and Larimer was a gathering place for Denver's elite, particularly during the 1890s. The "Windsor Hotel crowd" was a term broadly applied to the free-spending throng that dashed about the city in costly carriages and fancy buggies. The Windsor was torn down in 1961, just before Denver's emerging preservation conscience might have saved it from the wrecking ball. This photograph was taken in October 1947.

The Salvation Army building, located at 1841 Curtis Street, offered parking for fifteen cents a day when this photograph was taken on May 24, 1942.

During a Community Chest campaign, I took this photograph looking west down Sixteenth Street from California Street.

Thousands of north Denver residents used the Fourteenth Street viaduct when driving to and from downtown every day. Note the motorcycle officers directing traffic.
May 5, 1948.

The Albany Hotel at Seventeenth and Stout streets once housed KFEL Radio and the A. G. Clarke Drug Company.

I took this photograph from the roof of the City and County Building looking east to the Cathedral of the Immaculate Conception, the Colorado State Capitol building, and the Colorado Department of Revenue building on the right.

◀ *This wintery view from the Colorado State Capitol shows the Civic Center, the City and County Building, and the old Denver Public Library. November 5, 1946.*

◀ *This view is to the right (north) of the one above it and shows the intersection of Broadway and Colfax as well as the blocks where the Hilton Hotel was built. The only tall building visible downtown was the Telephone Company Building. November 5, 1946.*

Until 1952, the Rocky Mountian News *was located at 1720 Welton Street. Next door was the Baker Hotel and the Arcade Grill and Billiard Hall. More than a few of us occasionally sneaked in for a shot— pool or otherwise—between assignments.*

The Denver City and County Building is decorated for the Christmas 1951 holidays. In the top photo, the Old Forester bottle can be seen off to the right.

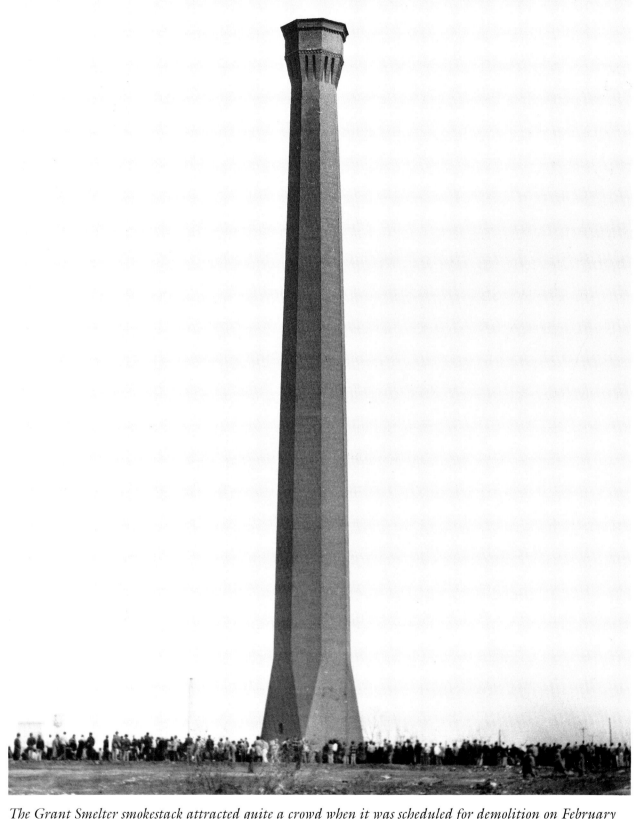

The Grant Smelter smokestack attracted quite a crowd when it was scheduled for demolition on February 25, 1950. I set up a series of four cameras and captured the sequence on the following page of the stack going down.

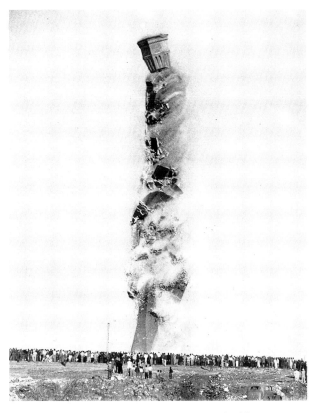

The stately landmark shatters from the blast . . .

and starts to fall . . .

into a pile of rubble . . .

leaving only a sliver.

As you can see, when the dust from the explosion of the Grant Smelter smokestack had cleared, there was a long sliver still standing. All of the news and radio personnel packed up and left. Gene Amole and I were talking while he packed up his radio gear, when all of the sudden there was a sharp, cracking sound and the balance of the stack started to fall. I turned on reflex and snapped the picture of it going down. I was the only one to get the shot. Amazingly enough, everyone is running on his right foot.

Here I am with my camera set-up for the demolition sequence. ▶

The Old Forester whiskey bottle was erected in December 1951 atop the Zook Building at Tremont Place and West Colfax as an advertisement by Brown-Forman Distillers of Louisville, Kentucky. The city fathers received so much criticism that it was subsequently removed on March 5, 1952.

The Old Forester bottle caused quite an uproar in town during the brief time it sat atop the Zook Building. Everyone had an opinion about the appropriateness of the bottle attracting such attention above Denver's skyline. *Rocky Mountain News* editor Jack Foster even claimed that the bottle was going to block his view of Longs Peak from the new *News* Building on West Colfax. Sam Lusky, then a writer for the *News,* had been "hitting the bottle" pretty hard in his column, and when Foster asked if anyone had an idea for a new angle for a bottle story, Sam said that it might be fun to climb up inside the bottle and get a different view. Foster thought it was a great idea and said, "Take Engle with you." We ended up climbing the girders on the inside of the bottle—it was sixty-seven and one-half feet tall. Sam and I both got stuck crawling through the neck, but we managed to pull through the top—no cork, just an open lid—and I got my pictures for Sam's story, even with the bottle swaying in the wind.

The Cosmopolitan Hotel, in the far background, and the Shirley-Savoy Hotel at Seventeenth and Broadway were long-time Denver landmarks. In between is the Mile High Center, which was one of the tallest buildings in Denver at the time of this 1955 photograph.

On May 26, 1954, I photographed the changes taking place on Denver's skyline. The top view looks east from lower downtown to the Denver Club Building, left, and the Mile High Center under construction. Pictured below, in the foreground, is the Denver Club Building under construction and at left center is the Kittridge Building with Denver Dry Goods directly behind it.

The Petroleum Club Building was the scene of many oil and gas deals as a number of local oil and gas companies came of age in the 1950s. It was also the home of Columbia Savings. September 15, 1957.

As a youngster, I attended Cub Scout meetings at the Capitol Heights Presbyterian Church at Eleventh Avenue and Fillmore Street.

Shorter A.M.E. Church was located at Cheyenne Place and Twenty-third Street.

What started out to be a routine photograph of the Central Christian Church at 1600 Lincoln turned into an amusing picture of the church sign resting atop a "One Way, Do Not Enter" sign. April 3, 1950.

East Denver High School at Sixteenth Avenue and Esplanade has graduated tens of thousands of Denver residents, including me.

This night photograph of the Public Service Company Building (left) and the Telephone Company Building (right) was taken from the Daniels & Fisher Tower. February 27, 1949.

The view below of Sixteenth Street was also taken from the Daniels & Fisher Tower.

This picture was made while the General Rose Memorial Hospital, located at 900 Clermont Street, was undergoing construction. February 17, 1948.

Bella Vita Towers was surrounded by vacant fields at South Colorado Boulevard and Interstate 25 when it was built in October 1964.

The Montgomery Wards *store on South Broadway at Virginia, built in 1929, was a Denver landmark for* decades until it was demolished by one giant implosion in 1993.

◄ *The* Rocky Mountain News *building at 400 West Colfax Avenue had just been completed when this photo was made on June 2, 1952.*

◄ *The May D&F store at Sixteenth Street and Tremont Place and the Hilton Hotel at Sixteenth and Cleveland Place quickly became downtown landmarks.*

I made this aerial photo of the Grant Smelter stack and Miller's Super Market warehouse just a few days before the stack's demolition in February 1950.

In this aerial view of the Denver Union stockyards about 1946, the Union stockyards building is in the center and just to the right is the oval arena building. The cattle pens and Armour and Company are in the background.

Many a Denver youngster had his or her first dining experience in the Denver Dry Goods Tea Room with mother and grandmother. It was a Denver institution for decades until it finally closed on March 14, 1987. During the Christmas season, Santa Claus arrived to pass out gifts to children whose parents had brought them to the annual Christmas party. The main dining room was set with child-size tables and chairs, and ice cream, cookies, and tea were served in delicate china cups, saucers, and plates, with small silverware to match, all of which the children got to keep.

This 1946 aerial shows the State Capitol and the City and County Building and downtown Denver. The Daniels & Fisher Tower is still the tallest building in town.

This skyline view of Denver was taken March 1964 and shows the Y.M.C.A. Building in the foreground and, from left to right, the Majestic Building, the Security Life Building just being completed, Western Federal Building, First National Bank Building, and the Mile High Center.

A view of the western skyline of downtown shows, from left to right, the Petroleum Club Building, the Hilton Hotel, the Majestic Building (center), Security Life Building, Western Federal Building, First National Bank Building, and the Brown Palace Hotel.

Half buried under a pall of smoke lies Denver, with many of the buildings obscured by the thick cloud of smog encircling the city. This picture was made at 9:00 AM on January 12, 1950.

THREE

HARRY, IKE, &
THE POLITICS
OF THE TIMES

I took freelance photographs for Mayor Ben Stapleton's 1939 campaign, but my first baptism in presidential politics occurred in 1947 during a visit to Denver by President Harry Truman. Reporter Duncan Clark and I were assigned to cover the President's speech at the State Capitol at 10:00 AM. We were supposed to be there by 9:00, but when I got to Clark's, he was still in the bathtub nonchalantly reading a book. I hustled him up and we hurried down to the Capitol only to find it almost deserted.

For security reasons, the secret service had rescheduled the event for Fitzsimons Army Hospital. We tore out East Colfax and got through the gate at Fitz just as it was closing. I grabbed my camera, jumped out of the car, rushed through a semi-circle of other newspeople, and suddenly found myself confronting Harry himself in an open limosine. Immediately, two secret service agents grabbed me by the collar and literally lifted me off the ground. I must have looked pretty surprised, because the President, in his clipped Missouri accent said, "Hold on, boys. Put him down. What would you like, son?" After stammering some excuse about being late because of the rescheduling, I said that I'd like to take his picture. "Anything you want, son," he replied. I felt ten feet tall as I got the best close-up of any photographer that day.

President Harry S. Truman speaks to personnel at Fitzsimons Army Hospital in 1947. ▶

President Truman visited Denver in October 1952 while campaigning for Adlai Stevenson. The Truman motorcade led a parade up Sixteenth Street. With the President in the black Cadillac were U.S. Senator Edwin C. Johnson, center, and former Colorado Governor Lee Knous. I rode on the Truman train that October as the President whistle-stopped his way across Colorado. By the time we reached Salida, Mr. Truman was dead tired. As he appeared on the back of the observation car to greet the crowd, Darlene Donahoo, the mascot of the Salida High School Marching Band, climbed the steps and presented him with a bouquet of flowers. I asked Mr. Truman if he would mind lifting her up for a picture. As tired as he was, he managed to pick her up and smile. His daughter, Margaret, is on the right. October 7, 1952.

President Truman and his daughter, Margaret, wave to the crowd from the rear platform of the presidential special in Grand Junction. October 7, 1952.

Despite Truman's campaigning for Stevenson, too many people liked Ike, including these folks displaying a banner over the Truman special.

Ike didn't always smile at me. During the 1952 campaign, Mr. Eisenhower had his headquarters at the Brown Palace Hotel. A controversy arose concerning a letter from John Foster Dulles, Ike's future secretary of state. I asked Jim Haggarty, Ike's press secretary, if I could get a picture of Ike with the letter. Haggarty said no, but I obtained a couple of sheets of paper from the Brown's public stenographer and approached several members of the New York delegation. "How would you like to have your picture taken with Ike?" I asked. "Just stand real close to him and hold the paper in front like you're conferring." Ike caught on, so I asked again if he would mind if I took a picture of him supposedly reading the letter in question. He blew up and said, "That's absurd and out of character, you son-of-a-bitch." To which I replied, "So is running for president, you son-of-a-bitch." Needless to say, I was soon told to report back to the office immediately. For a long time thereafter, my only assignments with Ike consisted of going to Lowry Air Force Base and watching his plane take off and land. I was to have no contact with him and was to go to work only if the plane crashed.

Ike had strong ties to Denver. Mamie's mother, Elivera Doud, lived at 750 Lafayette Street and he was a frequent visitor to the home, including this particular afternoon when he greeted a group of neighborhood children. August 28, 1953.

President Eisenhower gingerly tastes the top of a sugar beet during a visit to a farm near Brighton. September 14, 1954.

Republican Wendall Wilkie campaigned unsuccessfully against President Franklin D. Roosevelt in the 1940 election. Here Wilkie waves to a crowd in front of the Antlers Hotel in Colorado Springs in 1940.

First Lady Eleanor Roosevelt arrives at Denver Municipal Airport. Note the lack of buildings in the background.

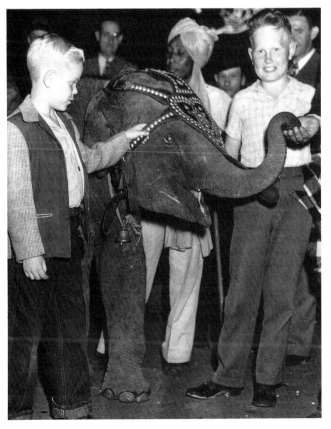

Thomas E. Dewey was probably the coldest, most obnoxious politician I ever met. It was no surprise to me that Harry Truman beat him. In fact, I made money betting on Truman because of an incident at the Brown Palace Hotel. Dewey had an elephant named Little Eva traveling with him. Pocky Marranzino and I took four kids from the Denver Orphans Home down to see her. Since the Denver Zoo did not have an elephant, the kids composed a letter asking Mr. Dewey to donate Little Eva to the Denver Zoo. When they set out to deliver it, they encountered New York State troopers and police at every turn. Finally, Pocky and I suggested that they go to the presidential suite floor. When Dewey emerged from his suite, the kids rushed up to him with their letter. He started to push them away, but then saw my camera. He managed a half-hearted glance at the letter, but as he pushed his way past Pocky and me, he said, "You sons-of-bitches." At that point, I knew he would never be president.

U. S. Senator Edwin C. Johnson and former Colorado Governor Lee Knous stand with President Harry Truman aboard the presidential special in Denver on October 7, 1952.

Ralph Carr, Colorado governor from 1939 to 1943, drew criticism for his defense of the rights of Japanese-Americans during World War II.

From 1933 to 1957, Edwin C. Johnson served Colorado first as governor, then U.S. senator, and again as governor.

All available seats in the House of Representatives chamber were taken as newly elected Colorado Governor Lee Knous was sworn in and delivered his inaugural address. January 15, 1947.

Congressman-elect John A. Carroll celebrates his election victory with his wife and daughter on November 6, 1946.

Denver Mayor Ben Stapleton makes a point during a lively speech in front of the City and County Building.

The election of Quigg Newton as mayor of Denver represented a changing of the guard in Denver politics. Here, Newton gets his cast autographed at a meeting at the Civic Center. The mayor had suffered a badly sprained ankle.

Eugene Cervi, publisher of Cervi's Journal, *ran unsuccessfully against Ed Johnson for the 1948 Democratic U.S. Senate nomination.*

Cervi forces show their support for their candidate during the 1948 State Democratic Convention.

Daniel M. (Danny) Sullivan, one-time Denver sheriff, Cripple Creek postmaster, and a staunch Republican, was a familiar figure on Seventeenth Street. Not wanting to have his picture taken, he threw a chair at me the minute after this shot was taken.

Dan Thornton, Jessie Thornton, and Donald Brotzman share a moment at the opening for the Citizens for Thornton campaign headquarters on August 28, 1956, as the former Colorado governor launched an unsuccessful attempt to win a seat in the U.S. Senate.

Dan Thornton surveys his herd of Herefords on his ranch near Gunnison during his campaign for the U.S. Senate.

Colorado politics 1950s style—rancher Governor Dan Thornton with his dog and pickup.

FOUR
WINGING THROUGH THE SKIES

The Army Air Corps taught me to fly during World War II, but shortly after receiving my wings, I was assigned to the Photo School instructors class at Lowry Field because of my knowledge of photography. It was the beginning of an exciting marriage of my twin passions—flying and photography. Little did I know at the time how important flying, and my ability to get the special view from the air, would be to my photographic career. As far as I know, there were no other newspaper photographers in the country at the time who filled both pilot/photographer status.

Once, in the middle of my vacation, I got a call from the city editor to pack my gear and hop a flight for Winslow, Arizona, after two airliners collided over the Grand Canyon. None of the airline people would give me the time of day. Finally, I found out the approximate location of the wreckage and called a friend in Phoenix, who knew a guy who rented airplanes, and I had him fly a Cessna 182 to Winslow for me.

At sunup, I took off for the crash site, and after dropping into the canyon, I spotted the wreckage and made my pictures. Climbing out of the canyon proved a bit slow, however, and suddenly around a cliff came a SA-16 rescue aircraft heading straight for me. Knowing that I didn't have the power to pull up and dodge him, I tried to dive beneath him. The SA-16 pilot must have had the same thought because, with more power, he pulled back on the stick and went above me. Fortunately, we passed with room to spare, and I was all too glad to have a few snorts on the way back to Denver with Frontier Airlines doing the flying.

A Trans World Airlines (TWA) DC-4 awaits its passengers at Denver Municipal Airport. May 9, 1940. ▶

The Civil Air Patrol (CAP) was organized as a civil defense unit on January 12, 1941. The Colorado Wing was originally stationed at the old Walt Higley Airfield at Twenty-sixth and Oneida. In 1943, the wing moved its operations to Denver Municipal Airport. Above, the Colorado Wing is ready for inspection at Denver Municipal. Below, volunteer members move an old building to a foundation for use as a CAP office building.

I learned to fly in this Piper L-4, sometimes called the Piper Cub J-5. It had a Continental 75 hp engine and was used for primary flight training in the early days of the war.

The Waco UPF-7 biplane was used to teach secondary flight training for all types of acrobatics. It had a 220 hp engine. April 15, 1943.

The Link Instrument Trainer was used to train pilots for instrumental flying. This one was at Huron, South Dakota, and when you squeezed into the cockpit and closed the hood, it was like sitting in a little dark box. December 16, 1943.

The Culver Cadet was made totally out of plywood, carried two persons, and had retractable landing gear that was operated by a hand crank.

The Waco cabin biplane, model YKS, was used in instrument training. July 8, 1943.

Above, a Waco biplane pulls a glider aloft from a dirt strip atop North Table Mountain. Below, the glider soars over Golden and North Table Mountain.

The B-17 was America's premiere heavy bomber in the early days of World War II. These early model Y1-B-17s were parked at Lowry Field.

The B-29 Superfortress carried the burden of long-range bombing raids against Japan. These B-29s were parked at Lowry Field.

Armed Forces Day at Lowry Air Force Base featured a full line of aircraft on display for the public, including a C-24 cargo plane, foreground, and B-47 and B-36 bombers.

The B-47 was the air force's first jet bomber and the backbone of the Strategic Air Command during the early 1950s.

Denver Municipal Airport was renamed Stapleton Airport after Denver Mayor Ben Stapleton in 1944. This photograph shows Denver Municipal with the hangars on the left and the administration building on the right. The control tower was on the second floor on the east side of the building.

A United Airlines DC-3 comes in to land at Stapleton Airport as disc plows are turning the rich soil between the runways. McIlvaine Farms planted 1,240 acres of wheat on airport ground under contract to the City and County of Denver. Now that was really the good old days! November 6, 1947.

Clinton Aviation was an early fixed base operator at Denver Municipal Airport after World War II. A Cessna twin and a Cessna 140 are parked in front of the Clinton hangar.

Units of the fighter wing of the Colorado National Guard stand in formation at Buckley Naval Air Station, as they are transferred from a guard unit to the regular air force. April 1, 1951.

A Continental Airlines DC-3 is parked in front of hangar six at Denver Municipal Airport. The DC-3 was the workhorse of both military and civilian transport in the late 1930s and 1940s and for many years thereafter in some parts of the world.

A Continental Airlines Convair 580 flies over the plains east of Denver. The Convair 580 was a regular on routes throughout Colorado well into the 1980s.

Public Service Company of Colorado's DC-3 takes on passengers at Denver Municipal Airport.

A United Airlines DC-6 made a belly landing at Denver Municipal Airport. October 21, 1947.

Mr. and Mrs. Eugene Ward stand in front of their picket fence at 1620 Verbana Street after a twin engine C-46 crashed in an adjoining vacant lot. The plane's nose bellied up to the fence but did not break it. Another fifty feet and the plane would have been in their house. Miraculously, there were no injuries. July 30, 1950.

An engine on an American Airlines DC-6 tore loose from its mountings and sent the propeller slicing through the top of the cabin. These photographs were taken moments after the plane landed at Stapleton Airport. August 22, 1950.

Fire Captain Barney Chamberlain of Engine Company Twenty-two examines gasoline dripping from the severed fuel lines. ▶

Stewardess Margaret Peterson stands in the door with one of the fifty-six persons who brushed with death on board the plane. ▶

The tail section of the DC-3 was the largest piece of wreckage intact. January 31, 1946.

Early one morning in January 1946, before I was hired by the *News,* I received a call from Harold Heroux of International News, asking me to cover a United Airlines DC-3 crash on Elk Mountain, Wyoming. I drove to the scene with the temperature thirty degrees below zero and a thirty-mile-an-hour wind howling. Fortunately, Harold had told me to take snowshoes and heavy clothes. Less than twenty-four hours after the crash, I reached the 11,162-foot summit of the peak in blizzard conditions along with army rescue personnel and three other news people. I shot my pictures and was ready to leave via the steep side of the mountain, but the army refused, citing "safety" reasons. Finally, they agreed to let me descend the steep slopes if I would pull two of the bodies to the bottom. I did, and that gave me a four-hour head start back to Denver. The other news people were required to take the same route down as we had come up. Consequently, my photos were the first on the wire out of Denver.

Later, bodies were brought out on dog sled. February 3, 1946.

A rescue worker searches the wreckage. Most of the twenty-one people on board were military personnel going home. January 31, 1946.

Captain Mary Parker Converse of Denver, left, held a master's certificate for ocean-going yachts and was entitled to wear the officer's jacket with master's four gold stripes while in her seventies. Her granddaughter, Dianna Converse, took her grandmother's enthusiasm for adventure into the skies. October 3, 1947.

Dianna Converse, Captain Mary's granddaughter, married Captain John Cyrus, an army pilot from Fort Worth, Texas, in 1943. Dianna became interested in flying and learned to fly in October 1943. Cyrus was shot down and killed during the Battle of the Bulge in December 1944, but Dianna didn't quit flying. She bought a surplus A-26, the type of aircraft in which her husband was killed, and Paul Mantz, adviser to Amelia Earhart and well-known aerial photographer, taught her to fly it. Dianna broke the Los Angeles to Denver speed record with a time of two hours, nineteen minutes, and twenty seconds. October 3, 1947.

I used a Hughes 300 helicopter on some of my photo assignments.

The first jet engine helicopter, the Alouette, was made by the French and first flown in Denver by Hersey Young of Helicopters, Inc.

An S-51 Sikorsky helicopter gave a demonstration at Lowry Field on Armed Forces Day.

The Alouette demonstration took place at Stapleton. Later, the Alouette played an important role in search and rescue and fire fighting operations.

*A French Caravelle jet visited Stapleton as part of a tour of demonstration flights for the airline industry.
I flew to California on board it and got to take the controls for awhile. What a great plane! June 1957.*

*The Boeing 707 was to jet travel what the DC-3 had been to the age of propellers. The 707 made its debut in
Denver in front of Continental hangar two at Stapleton on February 13, 1957.*

An F-104 Starfighter was on display at Lowry Air Force Base on Armed Forces Day.

A flight of F-84F jet fighters, flown by the famed Air Force Thunderbirds, takes off from Lowry Air Force Base as part of an Armed Forces Day program in 1955 or 1956.

Stapleton International Airport continued to be expanded even after the decision was made to build a new airport. This photograph showing a lack of travelers in the main terminal was taken on June 9, 1989, during the debate about building Denver International Airport.

A Cessna 310 flies over downtown Denver with the Western Federal Building, the new Federal Building, and the First National Bank Tower visible. The tip of the Daniels & Fisher Tower is visible above the plane's fuselage and the Hilton Hotel is at the extreme right. October 28, 1964.

This aerial of Stapleton Airport from the west was made on June 10, 1955.

FIVE

DENVER
PLAYS
HARD, TOO

When it comes to favorite pastimes, I've got to put fishing right up there on the top of the list. Unfortunately, the *News* didn't have much of a demand for fishing photographs, but I did cover just about every other sport and recreational event around. Some of my favorite photos show a bunch of kids—the infamous "Knot Hole Club"—watching a baseball game at old Merchants Park.

One of my regular assignments during the fall was to cover the University of Wyoming football games in Laramie. The problem was that I had to leave Denver by 9:00 AM, drive to Laramie, and then I could only stay for the first quarter in order to get back to Denver in time to develop and print for the early edition. Unbeknownst to the *News*, I solved the problem by renting an airplane and flying to Laramie. That way, I didn't have to leave Denver until 11:00 AM and I could stay at least until halftime. After flying back to Denver, I even had time for dinner at home before driving to the paper and getting there at the same time as if I'd made the whole drive to Laramie. I made an extra $3 on my expense account, because renting the plane was cheaper than my mileage rate for the drive. No one at the *News* bothered to ask how I was getting all of the second quarter action!

The Boys of Summer—Merchants Park in the 500 block of South Broadway was Denver's baseball field before the days of Mile High Stadium. The "Knot Hole Club" was for youngsters who didn't have the price of admission. The kids would look through holes in the fence and sometimes, if there were empty seats, be allowed in without charge. July 19, 1948. ▶

Catcher Bill Edwards of the Denver Bears refuses to give an inch while blocking the plate, and here his work kept George Verespy of the Colorado Springs Sky Sox from scoring. Verespy tried to score from third when Buddy Phillips sent a dribble down the first base line. April 19, 1950.

The "Knot Hole Club" kids catch a glimps of a game. July 19, 1948. ▶

The new Denver Bears Stadium was almost complete in August 1948. It later became Mile High Stadium after additional seating was added for football games.

Monte Irvin, star outfielder of the New York Giants, broke his ankle sliding into third during an exhibition game at Bears Stadium. Monte ended up in a local hospital with his leg in a cast. April 3, 1952.

"Babe" Didrikson Zaharias, one of the greatest athletes of the first half of the twentieth century, roared from behind on the back nine to enter the finals of the Women's Western Golf Tournament at Cherry Hills. June 24, 1950.

*Right on the old snozzle. The recipient of a straight right from southpaw Lou Rulon was Ralph Bollinger,
Denver University, in a stirring featherweight battle in the Elks Punch Bowl. Rulon won the match with
punches such as these.*

"Whoops, I should have ducked," seems to be the expression on the face of Art Henz after being floored by Melvin Geiche in a rousing welterweight battle on the opening card of the News-Elks Tournament. Geiche won by a TKO in the third. January 20, 1948.

A News-Elks Golden Gloves Tournament shows Bill Kinney, Seattle Fish Company entrant, landing a punch from underneath to the jaw of Joe Troyon of Camp Carson. January 24, 1950.

This cowboy made a perfect throw in his calf-roping attempt. The action was part of the opening of the Forty-sixth Annual National Western Stock Show and Rodeo being held for the first time in the new $3 million Denver Coliseum. January 12, 1952.

"He jumped on his horse and rode off in all directions," could describe this action as renowned rodeo clown, Buddy Heaton, heads off on a horse named El Rocco during the wild horse race at the National Western.

"Spur 'em high on the point!" This is the bronc-riding competition at the National Western.

Fishing on Evergreen Lake has always been a popular pastime.

*"Pardon my elbow, boy,"
says Clifford King of Hesston
Kansas Motors as he swats Tom
Jacquet of the Denver Chevs
and drives for the basket. The
Chevs finally won forty-nine to
forty-five. Take a look at those
shoes! March 23, 1950.*

*A crowd packs the University
of Denver Stadium to watch
football sometime during
the 1940s.*

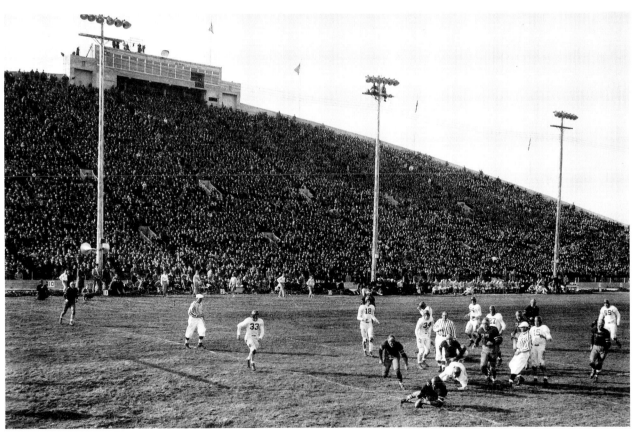

Lucky Lott, a daredeveil stunt driver, takes to the air before a crowd at the University of Denver Stadium.

Driver Willie Young and co-owner Roy Leslie admire the sleek V-8 Kenz-Leslie Special after its return to Denver from the Bonneville Salt Flats where it smashed all hot rod speed records. The record-smashing run by Young was 252.10 miles per hour. September 2, 1952.

Flying through the air with the greatest of ease, this young swimmer leaps off the diving board at Washington Park.

The East High School marching band performs at the D.U. Stadium in the fall of 1941.

The Beacon Supper Club on East Colfax Avenue was a popular spot for the comedy of the times. Club owners Gerry Bakke (with trombone) and Willie Hartzel (left) took part in the entertainment, accompanied by organist Patsy Hartzel.

A motorcycle officer and a parade of elephants led the Cole Brothers Circus into town from the train to the circus grounds at Thirty-eigth and York streets. August 3, 1947.

Denver's temperature was 94 degrees, but this camel didn't seem to mind. August 3, 1947.

The Berthoud Pass Ski Area was one of Colorado's earliest. This view shows the old rope tow and looks west across the summit of the pass. February 9, 1941.

In early 1940, I went with Paul Norine to the *Denver Post,* when he took some photographs to Joy Swift, the editor of the Sunday *Rotogravure* section. Paul introduced me to Miss Swift who was a delightful person. As time went by, I drove around the foothills and up to Berthoud Pass and Trail Ridge Road and made scenic photos. I took them to Miss Swift and, much to my surprise, she used a number of them in *Rotogravure* over a period of time. Over the years, I sold many photos to the *Post* until the *News* hired me.

Berthoud Pass Ski Area. February 9, 1941.

Winter Park Ski Area and the West Portal of the Moffat Tunnel about 1941.

This group of enthusiastic skiers are Rocky Mountain News *delivery boys on a ski train outing to Winter Park.*

Skier Claudis Banks of Vernal, Utah, wasn't satisfied with the run of the mill daytime skiing. Stringing his gear with lights that would be the envy of any self-respecting Christmas tree, he demonstrated his nighttime skiing during the 1945 National Ski Tournament. Here he is shown in his electric regalia going full steam down Howelsen Hill at Steamboat Springs. The picture was made by a time exposure and setting off several large flash bulbs in various locations to bring out the trees and snow.

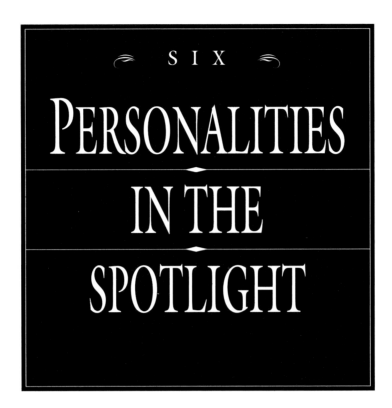

SIX

PERSONALITIES
IN THE
SPOTLIGHT

It was always interesting to me to be sent out to photograph celebrities—either Denver's own or those who came to town. Sometimes I had the opportunity for little more than a polite nod over my flashgun, but other times we would end up having quite a conversation. Most were very congenial—not at all stuck on themselves—and they were usually more than willing to cooperate for a photograph that was going to give them publicity.

Once, when Doris Day and Bob Hope came to Denver to promote funding for the Denver Area Community Chest, I was sent out to make some photographs. Not surprisingly, I found my camera lens focusing on Doris much more than on Hope. Besides, it seemed to me that Hope was trying to grab the spotlight too much. He was still on his way up in those years. When I got back to the paper and developed a set of Doris Day photos, the editor blew his top and sent me back with instructions to "get back there, and get some of Bob Hope, too!"

Doris Day, singer and actress, entertains at a Denver Area Community Chest fund drive at the Denver Auditorium. October 12, 1948. ▶

General Douglas MacArthur posed for a photograph with two local admirers at Stapleton Airport on November 13, 1951, six months after he was relieved of his command in Korea by President Truman.

Anthony Eden, then British foreign secretary, visited Denver on August 5, 1951.

Eddie Bohn, Denver restaurateur and boxer, was also Colorado state boxing commissioner.

Arthur M. Oberfelder was a well-known Denver play promoter and producer. May 15, 1950.

Sidney O. Lindahl, commonly known as "Sid," was the father of the best photo flash guns made. He invented the Heiland flash, which later became the "SOL" flash gun, and was able to synchronize both the old magnesium foil bulbs and later the wire-filled bulbs.

*America's biggest question mark romance—that of Jimmy Stewart and Gloria Hattrick McLean—
set hearts a flutter at Stapleton Airport when the couple drove to Denver from Colorado Springs to fly
to California. April 4, 1949.*

Rudy Vallee, well-known "crooner," singer, and recording artist, visited Denver with his wife and dog.
June 5, 1951.

John Bromfield, left, and Stan Jones, right, were in Denver to promote the television show Sheriff of Cochise, *when they stopped by Pete Smythe's general store at East Tin Cup on KOA radio.*

Gene Autry was the "Singing Cowboy" and appeared in many Westerns during the 1940s and 1950s.

Eddie Cantor, popular radio, television, and movie personality, visited Denver.

Benny Goodman, known as the "King of Swing" during the Big Band Era, on the right, and Sammy Kaye, another big band leader, were in Denver at the same time and took time out to clown around to promote the battle of the bands. Kaye's motto was "Swing and sway with Sammy Kaye."

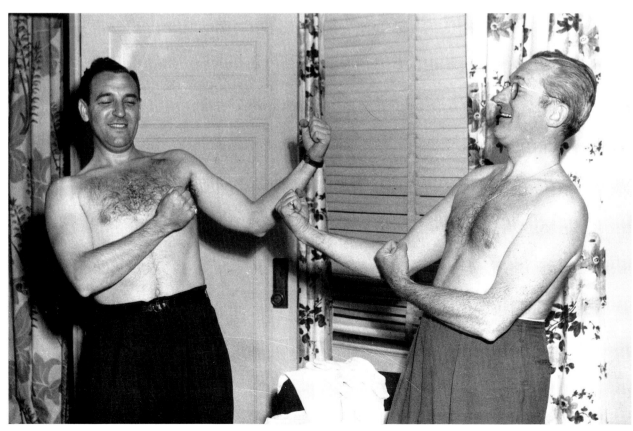

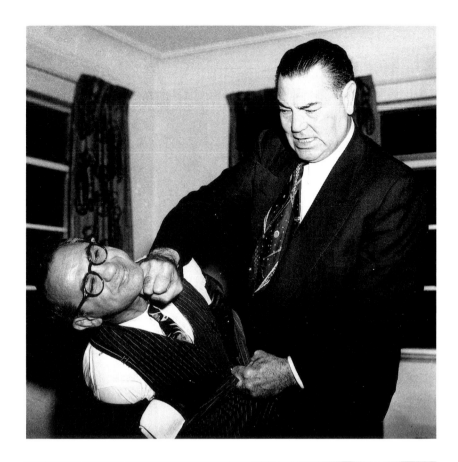

Jack Dempsey, former world heavyweight champion boxer clowns around and delivers a powerful right to Joe "Awful" Coffee, a long-time friend and prominent Denver restaurateur.

Denver Mayor Will Nicholson, center, and Palmer Hoyt, publisher of the Denver Post, *left, greeted ventriloquist Edgar Bergen who was in Denver doing a promotion for Bergen's television show,* Do You Trust Your Wife. *October 13, 1956.*

Rubinoff and his famous violin performed at a press conference for high school students.

Herndon Davis was a famous Colorado artist who painted many murals for the Colorado Historical Society.

Fred Arthur was an early disc jockey for radio station KTLN and had a program known as King Arthur's Court.

Jack Gilmore was a famous Denver private eye.

A very young Don Martin was a newscaster for radio station KTLN and was also known as the "Sky Spy" for his traffic reports from the air.

Tempest Storm, a nationally known stripper, came to Denver to perform at the Tropics Night Club on Morrison Road.

Harold Lloyd, actor and comedian, started out delivering the Rocky Mountain News *in 1909. When he returned with the Shriners convention in 1949, he autographed a score of copies of the newspaper which were sold by fellow Shriners to benefit Shriners Hospitals for Crippled Children. March 31, 1949.*

Carl Sandell was the doorman at the Daniels & Fisher store for most of his adult life. In many ways, he was more of a landmark in Denver than the tower itself.

Eventually, I did get some shots of Bob Hope, too, when Doris Day and Bob Hope came to Denver to promote funding for the Denver Area Community Chest. October 12, 1948.

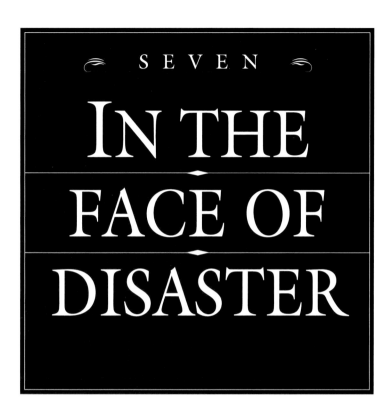

SEVEN

IN THE FACE OF DISASTER

A lot of my photographs may look pretty grisly to some, but that's the way we covered things in those days before television. The only difference now is that a TV crew rushes to the scene in a helicopter and gets the whole thing on video tape. It can be rather graphic that way, too, but somehow when you've got to tell the story with only one or two still pictures, they seem even more graphic.

Sometimes we were dispatched at all hours of the night when a story broke. Other times, I got the shot just because I was close by and had a camera in the car. That's what happened on December 4, 1951, when Jack Gaskie and I were returning to the office from a story down south. As we headed north on Santa Fe Drive, we saw a military aircraft flying low and slow to the east. I remarked to Jack, "That guy is having problems." As we approached Iowa Avenue, a call came over the police radio reporting a plane crash at Bayaud and Eudora streets. We took off at speeds up to fifty miles an hour and were the first newspeople on the scene. We were able to get some dramatic pictures before the fire department put out the flames.

◄ *Fire fighters battle the blaze from the crash of a B-29 bomber at Bayaud and Eudora streets. December 4, 1951.*

Home owners survey the devastation caused by the B-29 that crashed in east Denver in the Hilltop area, destroying five homes and damaging many others. Miraculously, no one on the ground was killed. Eight people were killed in the crash and seven injured. December 4, 1951.

◄ *Firemen poured water onto the blazing hulk of the B-29, which had been attempting to land at Lowry Air Force Base.*

◄ *The skeleton of the tail section of the huge B-29 was all that remained after the blaze was extinguished.*

On October 1, 1941, I was driving around with the police radio on when a call came in about an explosion near Seventh and Clermont streets. I rushed over and found the fire department frantically digging in a vacant lot for what they thought were a couple of kids buried in a cave-in after an explosion. One boy was badly burned and was taken to Denver General. A detective at the scene, Jack Hargraves, took a liking to me and told me to follow him to the hospital. There, he helped me get in and shoot pictures of the boy being treated. I went home, developed them, and took them down to the *Rocky Mountain News.* Associate Editor Lee Casey was working that Sunday and was elated to get the chance to buy the photos. Little did I know that a few years later when I returned from the Army Air Corps looking for a job, Mr. Casey would remember me from that Sunday and help me get a job.

Fourteen-year-old Jack Murfin was treated at Denver General. Left to right are Detective Jack Hargraves, Dr. Claude Harris, Patrolman James Day, and Dr. G. Myron Harrison.

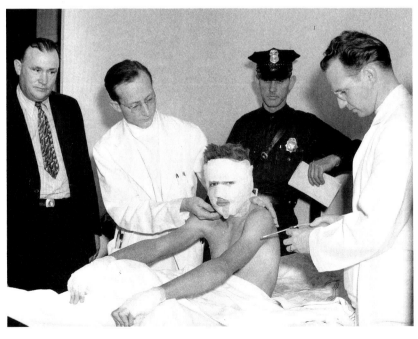

"Hay bombs away." After an early snowstorm, the crew of a C-47 loads hay and then prepares to drop the bales to starving cattle and sheep at the Keystone Ranch near Karval. November 13, 1946.

Being first to a news happening is sometimes pure luck. Sometimes, it practically happens in front of you. Duncan Clark and I were having coffee and doughnuts in a little greasy spoon across from an apartment building at 35 West Dakota Avenue when an explosion shattered the morning air. All I had to do was walk out to the car, get the camera, and go to work. I made these photographs of rescue crews beginning their long search for the dead and injured. May 31, 1947.

Destructive flood waters spread out over the countryside near Cambridge, Nebraska, when Medicine Creek flooded. June 22, 1947.

Telephone cable repairmen hang over the river on slings while tethered to land by a long safety rope.
June 22, 1947.

On June 22, 1947, Bob Perkin and I took off in a rented plane for Cambridge, Nebraska, the scene of a devastating flood that killed twelve people, injured others, and left many homeless. Upon arriving over Cambridge, I shot aerials and then needed to land. Cambridge had no airport, so I solved the problem by landing in an alfalfa field at the edge of town. We walked into town and got our story and then went back to the plane. Because of wind factors, I had to take off dodging haystacks. We ran short of fuel on the way back to Denver and landed at McCook to fuel up. Then, somewhere over eastern Colorado, our radio went dead and the navigation lights went out. We made it to Denver but could not contact the tower. I buzzed it with Bob waving a flashlight. Finally, the tower spotted us and killed all of the runway lights except the north/south runway and then gave us a green light to land. The most fun was scooping the other news people because I could set the plane down close to the flood area and get out in time to meet our deadline.

A sprawling mass of wreckage was all that was left of Yuma's railroad depot after a train derailed. Four persons were buried beneath the debris but miraculously escaped death. Once again, I managed to get several aerial views of the disaster. August 11, 1947.

Highway crews worked all night in the wake of three treacherous avalanches which closed U.S. 40 over Berthoud Pass. It was a typical late winter snow for Colorado which dropped many feet of heavy, wet snow. March 6, 1948.

A woman and her child found a restaurant closed due to the coal shortage that resulted when an early storm caught Denver unprepared and short on coal. The shortage caused heating problems for area hospitals and businesses as well as residences. November 16, 1946.

Another Colorado blizzard stranded travelers at Denver Union Station while trains vainly battled snowdrifts. Hundreds of travelers, some waiting more than twenty-four hours, anxiously waited for word about when they could continue on their way. January 3, 1949.

This was the aftermath of the January 1949 blizzard. Top, a cluster of vehicles was snowbound about six miles north of Nunn, Colorado. Bottom, this train was the first to move out of Nunn, taking stranded passengers to Denver. January 7, 1949.

A broken axle on Car No. 50
caused it to jump the track and
sideswipe Car No. 828. Note the
poster advertising basketball at
Mammoth Gardens. January
24, 1949.

This bread truck plunged
into the Platte River at West
Ohio and Valley Road after
it sideswiped a gravel truck.
Police reported that the truck
skidded 110 feet and knocked
out forty feet of guard rail
before going into the river.
July 18, 1949.

Firemen prepared to climb up the aerial ladder to the roof of the Barnes School of Commerce at 1440 Glenarm Place. Blinding smoke and searing flames repulsed fourteen companies of firemen for three hours in one of the worst fires downtown Denver ever had. March 28, 1948.

This fire occurred on Sixteenth Street during the Christmas season sometime during the late 1940s.

Aiming at the bullseye, a fireman jumps into a Browder net held by rookie firemen. Perfect form calls for the jumper to land on his seat with legs and upper body forming a 45-degree angle. These photos were made at the tower at Station No. 6 located at Thirteenth and Blake streets.

Rescue Squad No. 2 received a new truck in 1947. It's a far cry from the modern rescue units now in service.

Flames, fanned by high winds, engulfed barracks at Camp Carson south of Colorado Springs.

Only a skeleton remained after the fire left two dead and nine critically injured.

Frank Finn, one of the injured, read about the disaster in the Rocky Mountain News. *January 18, 1950.*

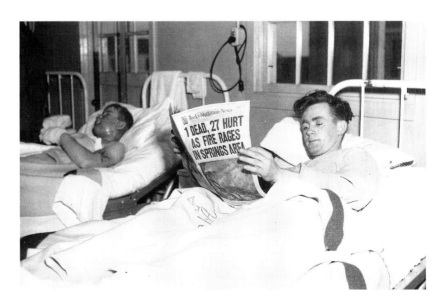

When a fire broke out at the Railroad Building at 1543 Larimer Street in 1956, firemen tried to break the three-quarter-inch plate glass windows. However, they didn't crack, but instead popped out of the frames in one piece and crashed to the sidewalk.

The Wolhurst Saddle Club at 8201 South Santa Fe Drive was one of Denver's swank establishments until a fire in the basement after a festive Saturday night crowd had departed turned the place to rubble. Two employees of the club lost their lives and the fire caused an estimated $1 million in damage. February 18, 1951.

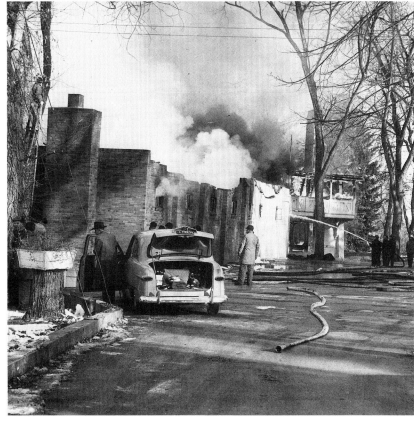

I got the call for the Wolhurst fire from Jack Foster, the News *editor, in the early hours of Sunday morning. I went over alone and started taking photographs of the fire. An instant after this photograph was taken, the giant brick chimney collapsed in a welter of flying bricks, smoke, and dust. February 18, 1951.*

This gap was left when huge Buckhorn Reservoir, six miles west of Loveland, lapped over its crest and then burst the dam to bring death and destruction down on Loveland. August 4, 1951.

Eight-inch slabs of pavement were tossed around like pebbles as flood waters roared through Big Thompson Canyon. This section of ripped highway extended two miles. August 4, 1951.

Automobiles were tossed around like sailboats by the flood waters. This Buick sedan was carried more than a quarter of a mile and sunk into the ditch. August 4, 1951.

Driftwood, telephone poles, power lines, fences, uprooted trees, and other debris were swept along by the giant waters of the flood which took seven lives. Eerily, the flood occurred almost exactly twenty-five years before the disastrous Big Thompson flood of 1976.

A sea of flames engulfed the Colorado Lumber Company at 3701 Wazee Street in a three-alarm fire that caused $175,000 in damage. The fire raced through the firm's factory, offices, and storage buildings and destroyed 500,000 feet of lumber before firemen could bring it under control. October 9, 1952.

Firefighters battle a two-alarm blaze at a warehouse at 2931 Blake Street, which raged out of control and threatened to destroy adjacent buildings. Twelve companies fought the blaze. November 16, 1952.

This wreck between a streetcar and auto occurred shortly after World War II. Note the War Chest poster on the streetcar.

This cement truck caught fire while en route to the plant. The fire was caused by faulty brakes and quickly spread to the cab of the tractor. The driver escaped with minor injuries.

Crushed metal was all that remained of the automobile in which a woman was killed when the car driven by her husband collided with the tender of a Burlington Northern switch engine less than a mile north of Denver on the old Brighton Road in 1945.

After a northwest Denver bar and restaurant was destroyed in an explosion, someone found a sign in the rubble that read "20% Cabaret Tax During Dancing Hours" and posted it as a joke.

This aerial view of Glenwood Springs shows the results of a major explosion and fire. The million-dollar fire, touched off by the explosion of two 20,000-gallon gasoline tanks, destroyed an entire city block and injured more than fifty people, twelve of them seriously. Note the old water tower on the mainline. May 16, 1948.

EIGHT

ON THE
CRIME
BEAT

I spent a lot of time on the police beat. I had quite a few friends on the force and usually we got along just fine. More than once, however, their police work and my journalistic pursuits collided.

On one such occasion, Al Nakkula and I were on our way to dinner when a call came in about a shooting in a house on Grant Street. We weren't far from the address, so we raced over and arrived before the police. We went in—maybe not too smart—and found a woman with a wound in the midsection lying on the floor. A man was standing beside her holding a .38 revolver. Not wanting to irritate him by taking picutres, I asked the fellow if he would mind giving me the gun. He handed it to me and admitted to the shooting. I started to take pictures just as the police arrived. Captain Connie O'Farrell immediately cussed me out for having the gun in my hands, saying that I had ruined the fingerprints. I told him that the man had admitted the shooting—this was long before the days of *Miranda* warnings—and that I felt a whole lot better having the gun than letting the shooter keep it.

Mr. Angel was carrying money to the bank when he was accosted, robbed, and shot to death in the alley near the Barth Hotel. I was sitting in my dad's car outside his downtown office at the time and heard the report on the police radio I had installed in the car. I drove down to the scene and took several pictures, which I sold to the Denver Post. *This was my first murder case and it started my newspaper freelancing career. October 4, 1941.* ▶

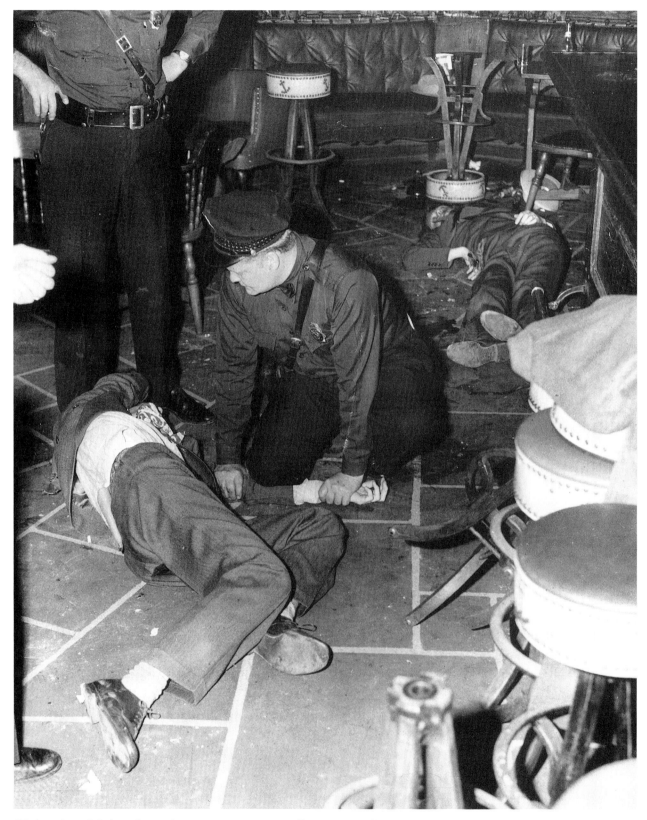

University of Colorado professor James Kane Mullin was fatally wounded in the Ship's Tavern of the Brown Palace Hotel on October 1, 1946, by Ronald Smith, who is being restrained by police.

A police surgeon attempts to aid Dr. Mullin as the bartenders look on, while Smith is being subdued by officer Bill Ohruh.

Jack Frank and I were at Twenty-second and Downing when the call came in that there had been a shooting at the Brown. We made it there in four minutes flat. In the meantime, Harriet Rhoads, now my wife, had rushed over from the office two blocks away and got the best shot of the melee and of the police subduing the shooter. Harriet started taking photos of witnesses when a fellow came up and tried to take her camera away. I went to her rescue and blocked his way, but we got into fisticuffs. He grabbed me by the back of my shirt collar and when I spun around, all I was wearing was the sleeves. He had ripped away the rest of my new gabardine shirt, at which point I gave him a clout with my flashgun. It turned out that the guy was upset because he shouldn't have been there with the person he was with.

The rape and murder of eighteen-year-old C.U. co-ed Theresa Catherine Foster in Boulder on the night of November 9, 1948, was the crime of the decade. Joe Sam Walker was convicted of the crime.

During the Theresa Catherine Foster murder case, not only were we out numbered by photographers and reporters from the *Denver Post*, but the paper had even hired Erle Stanley Gardner, well-known mystery writer, to go to Boulder and help solve the case. It was impossible to get any information out of the sheriff's office because he was friendly with the *Post*. One *Post* reporter followed us everywhere to see what progress we were making. One night, Jack Mohler and I ducked the guy and went to the coroner's office where we found a basement window open and climbed in. We found the gun and some bloody clothing, made our pictures, and got out. Needless to say, the *Post* was infuriated because they thought the coroner had made it all possible.

We still couldn't get any information from the sheriff's office, so we went to a fellow I knew a short distance from the courthouse who had a radio repair and electronics shop. He loaned me a set of earphones, a condenser, some alligator clips, and some wire. The telephone terminal box was in the men's lavatory. I clipped into the sheriff's lines and ran the wire into one of the stalls where I sat and listened for awhile. Jack Mohler stood outside and whistled whenever anyone approached. We got our story in spite of all the road blocks.

After twenty-five years of self-imposed exile, eighty-year-old oil tycoon Henry M. Blackmer arrived at Denver Union Station with his son, Myron. Blackmer was a central figure in the Tea Pot Dome investigation of the 1920s and charges of income tax evasion had been pending against him since 1928. September 26, 1949.

The Colorado State Penitentiary in Cañon City was the scene of a major jail break in 1948 when twelve convicts escaped through the north gate in a short-lived and unsuccessful bid for freedom. December 31, 1948.

At the end of December 1948, Dan Cronin and I were sent to Cañon City to cover the prison break. Again, we were out numbered by the *Post*, which had four photographers and four reporters covering the story. Fortunately, Warden Roy Best felt sorry for us. He gave us innumerable tips, one of which got us in the middle of a shootout between the guards and the escaped convicts. We had been told that if we drove with two of the prison guards on the search, they would have a good idea where the hideout was. We arrived in the vicinity of an old trailer shack, and when we got out of the car, all of a sudden the shooting began. Dan and I dropped down and crawled under the car. The guards fired with deadly accuracy and it was over in a minute. One convict was dead and the other captured.

Orville Turley, a fifty-four-year-old Denver murderer, lies dead in the snow outside a trailer east of Cañon City, where he was killed by a shotgun blast through the trailer window. Seconds later, Richard F. Heilman, who was wounded by another blast, emerged from the trailer. The story at the time was that Heilman held Turley in front of himself to keep from being hit by the first shot that killed Turley. December 31, 1948.

Another escaped convict, A. B. Tolley, a Moffat County murderer, froze both of his legs while hiding out and had to be assisted by a posse member.

Colorado State Penitentiary Warden Roy Best displays some of the handmade weapons the prisoners used in their escape. He is holding a phony sub-machine gun fashioned from wood, tape, and a length of pipe and knives made from tools stolen from the prison machine shop. December 31, 1948.

Warden Roy Best talks with John the "Eel" Smalley, after his recapture. December 31, 1948.

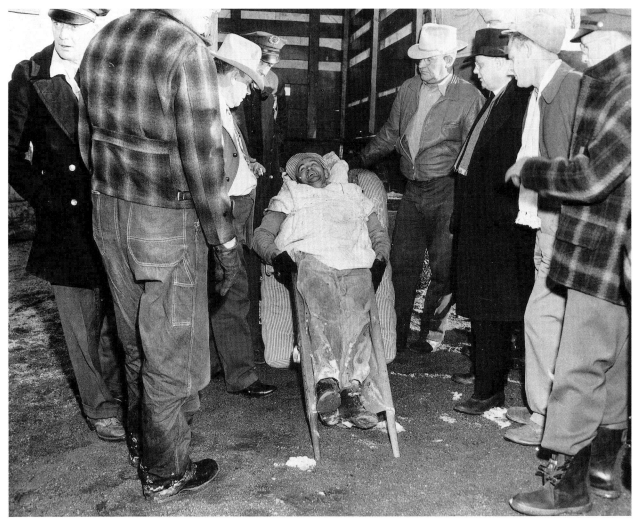

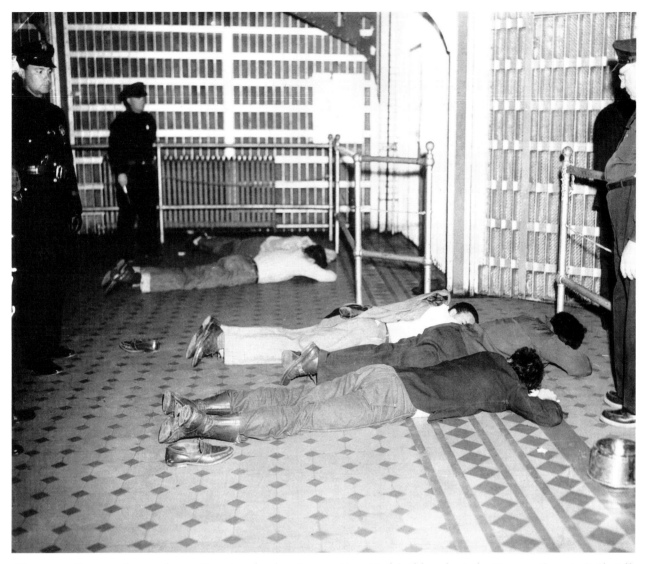

Denver police stand guard over five ring leaders in an attempted jail break at the Denver County Jail. All five were facing long prison terms and they faked a fight during church services to draw the guards into the cell blocks. Police responded to an alarm and quickly quelled the outbreak. April 24, 1950.

Fred Ward, left, was a prominent Denver automobile dealer, who built an empire selling Hudson cars—some more than once. Frederick Dickerson, right, was a veteran Denver defense attorney who represented Ward at his trial. This photograph was taken during a trial recess. The Ward case featured a bizarre sequence of events, including the discovery by Denver private eye Jack Gilmore of some of Ward's valuables hidden in a casket at Rogers Mortuary and the subsequent revelation that Ward had a past under a different name.

Fred Ward had quite a spread near Broomfield, which included an electrically heated horse barn for his race horses. At the ranch gate, News reporter Ken Wayman talks with a deputy sheriff. August 1, 1951.

Anthony Zarlengo, one of Fred Ward's attorneys, Iva Ward, and Fred Ward confer during Ward's trial. Ward was indicted by the grand jury on charges of false pretenses, confidence game, and conspiracy to commit both. He was found guilty on all counts. October 16, 1951.

Denver headlines were full of reports of gang warfare when thirty-year-old Mike Falbo, a long-time police character, was ambushed and slain about a mile east of Welby. Sheriff Homer Mayberry points to a bullet hole in the window of Falbo's automobile. January 8, 1948.

Police authorities were convinced that there was a link between the Falbo murder and the murder two years later of Harold "Murph" Cohen, a boxing promoter and gambler. Cohen's body was found at the bottom of Blue Lake, northwest of Denver, weighted down with two twenty-five-pound sections of railroad iron. Underworld rumors were that Cohen had been the "guest of honor" at a testimonial dinner the evening before. Neither murder was ever solved. February 11, 1950.

One of the sensational crimes of the 1950s occurred when John Gilbert Graham blew up a United airliner with forty-four persons on board, including his mother. His motive was the insurance money. Graham, in handcuffs, is led into Denver District Court for his trial. November 1955.

John Gilbert Graham, in handcuffs, confers with his attorneys, Charles Vigil, left, and John J. Gibbons.

John Gilbert Graham and his wife, Gloria, wait for court to go into session during Graham's trial.

I interviewed John Gilbert Graham at the Colorado State Penitentiary shortly before his execution.

On of January 12, 1957, shortly after I left the *Rocky Mountain News*, Bob Ajenian and Bill Hale, both from *Life* magazine, and I set out for the execution of John Gilbert Graham at the Colorado State Penitentiary in Cañon City. I had made a freelance deal with *Life* magazine that if I could get a picture of the execution, they would pay me $2,000. Bob had brought a miniature Minox camera with him to be used in the attempt. On the way, we stopped in Pueblo for a bite to eat and I purchased a package of Viceroy cigarettes. The "o" in Viceroy on the side of the package came at the exact spot where the camera lens was when inserted into the package. I carefully cut out the "o" and took out enough cigarettes to fit the camera snuggly in place. Then, I sealed the top of the pack so that a flap could be raised over the camera to trip the shutter and advance the film.

At the prison, we had to go through a metal detector. We emptied our pockets onto a shelf in the doorway next to the sensor. Bob went in front of me, so as he stepped through, I pushed the cigarette package into his belongings. When we were all inside, I asked Bob for a cigarette and he said, "Here, keep 'em. I have another pack."

While we were standing around waiting to be taken to the gas chamber, the warden decided that there should be a more thorough search. We had to empty our pockets and the guard checking me picked up the cigarette pack and noted that it was heavier than usual. He opened it and found the camera. The warden confiscated the camera but was still willing to let me go to the execution. I declined, however, stating that "I had come to do a job and if I couldn't, I had no desire to see a man die."

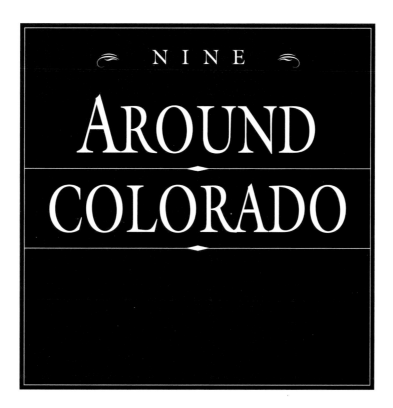

NINE

AROUND
COLORADO

Denver was certainly always my home base, but I did get around Colorado. In those days, even if you drove out to Red Rocks you felt like you had definitely left Denver because there was a lot of open countryside surrounding it in all directions. Today, the Front Range sprawl has blurred the distinctions between Denver and the surrounding suburbs.

I got around Colorado a lot on assignments, as you've already seen, but this book wouldn't be complete without just a few more photographs. Even if I was on a fishing trip or out with the family, I still had a camera in the car. More than once Harriet and the kids had to wait while Dad took a shot of something.

Frequently, I drove up Mount Evans, sometimes on a specific freelance assignment, other times just to poke around. Over the years, I sold a lot of scenery shots for postcards. I also spent time on the Western Slope doing freelance work for dude ranches and once did a spread for *Ford Times*. It was always different, and my time traveling around Colorado provided a nice change of pace from my reporting assignments.

◄ *The 1950s saw a changing of the guard in railroading—from the days of steam to the new era of diesels. This old watering tower on the outskirts of the railyards used to refill steam locomotives. The filler pipe and tank are adorned with the icicles that formed from the water leaking through the tank.*

These views show Red Rocks Park Amphitheater while undergoing construction and installation of the seats and stage about 1941. The rock formation encircling the amphitheater created a natural sounding board.

Easter sunrise services at Red Rocks Park have long been a tradition in Denver. I took this aerial shot from a Cessna 182. My normal procedure was to remove the righthand door before takeoff and put my camera in the right seat. From the lefthand pilot's seat, I would put the plane into a gentle bank and then lean over and shoot out the right door. The 182 was such a steady plane that unless the air was really choppy, this worked just fine.

Black Hawk has seen many changes, most notably a revival of gambling, since I took this picture of the Gilpin Hotel in 1946. I was hired to shoot publicity photos for the owner and one of the views she wanted was of her daughter taking a bath—covered with bubbles, of course—in one of the old-fashioned tubs.

Steamboat Springs had a ski area, but not much of one, when I took this picure in February 1945.

Anne Davis was a recluse who lived in a shack along Clear Creek. When the state started the new highway to Central City, Mrs. Davis attempted to stop the construction by firing 30.06 bullets that bounced off the Caterpillar blades and scared off the workmen.

Southwest Denver was dotted with small farm operations like this one near Littleton. This area is all developed now. February 15, 1941.

Magic Mountain was an Allen Lefferdink dream of a planned multi-million-dollar "Colorado Disneyland" on U.S. 40 in the foothills near Denver. A one-time builder, financier, Lefferdink's paper empire crumbled, leaving thousands of Colorado investors with worthless stock certificates. Heritage Square sits on this location today, but this work was done in the late 1950s long before I-70 was built through the Morrison hogback.

Colorado dude ranches have always been an important part of the state's tourist economy. Tourism boomed after World War II and visitors included this group of young ladies at the Drowsy Water Ranch at Hot Sulphur Springs, Colorado. Learning to milk the ranch's cows and brand cattle were part of the day's activities.

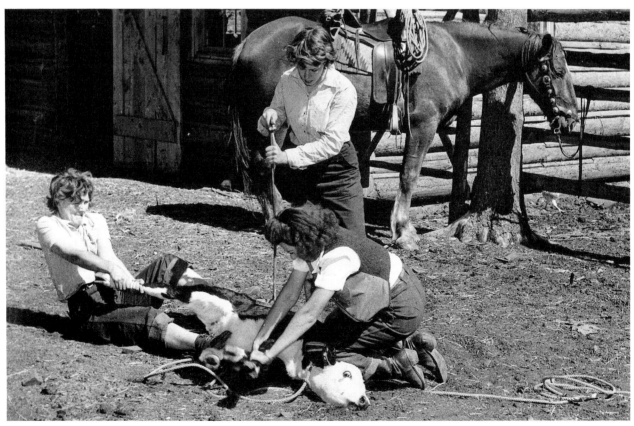

I left the *Rocky Mountain News* in 1956, but continued many freelance assignments. After a stint producing films for the Atomic Energy Commission and Martin Marietta, I started my own motion picture production company. As it turned out, the great Denver flood of 1965 was one of the events that marked the end of the postwar era in Denver. For all that I've photographed over the years, the one big event that's missing in my personal files is the 1965 flood. I was too busy being flooded out myself and trying to save equipment at Morey Engle Productions. The construction of the Eisenhower Tunnel was another of those events which seemed to say that things would never be the same along the Front Range of Colorado again. The first bore was opened in 1975, and I took this picture of construction in the second bore on July 11, 1978. I finally retired from my production company in 1986, and shortly got involved organizing my father-in-law's photographs for *Denver's Man with a Camera: The Photographs of Harry Rhoads.* Now that I have my own book done, I really am going to do nothing but go fishing. Course, I'll take my camera, just in case . . .

Index